Who were the Saxons?

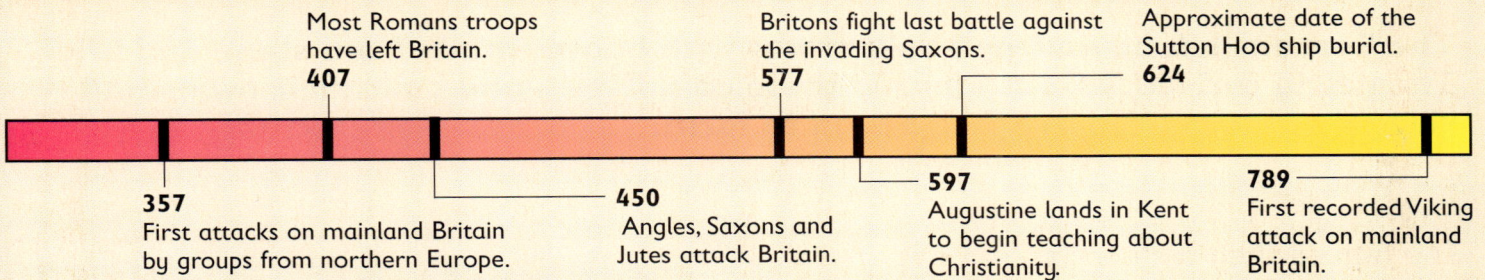

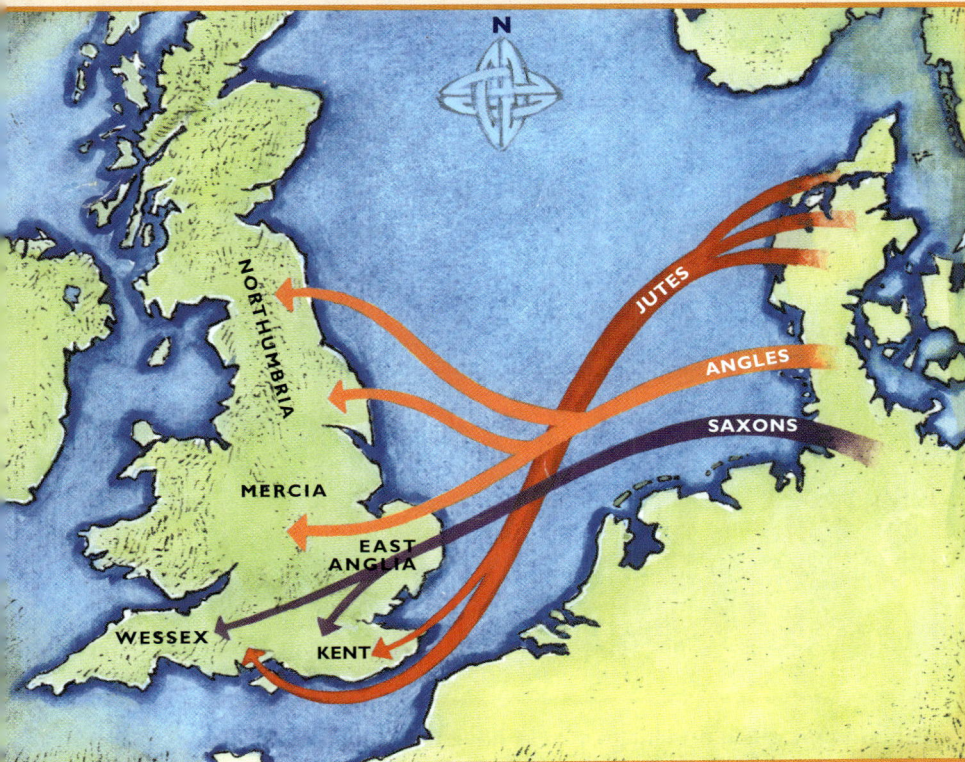

Most Romans troops have left Britain.
407

Britons fight last battle against the invading Saxons.
577

Approximate date of the Sutton Hoo ship burial.
624

357
First attacks on mainland Britain by groups from northern Europe.

450
Angles, Saxons and Jutes attack Britain.

597
Augustine lands in Kent to begin teaching about Christianity.

789
First recorded Viking attack on mainland Britain.

N

JUTES

ANGLES

SAXONS

NORTHUMBRIA

MERCIA

EAST ANGLIA

WESSEX

KENT

Did you know?

- Not all the Romans left suddenly. It is likely that many stayed, to continue living and farming in Britain.
- There have been several finds of buried Roman silver dating from this period. This suggests that some attacks were sudden and wealthy Romans hastily buried their wealth, hoping to return later.

After the Romans left Britain, different groups from northern Europe began to arrive in this country, some to steal and plunder, others in search of land to farm. Although we now call these invaders 'Saxons', they were, in fact, from three different tribes – the Angles from southern Denmark, the Saxons from northern Germany and the Jutes from northern Denmark. The map shows where these different groups settled.

In AD 357 Roman rule in Britain was challenged. In what seems to have been a co-ordinated attack, Picts from Scotland and Saxons from Denmark invaded by land and sea and succeeded in taking control of large parts of the country. It was not until the following year, under the skilful command of a Spanish general called Theodosius, that the Romans regained control.

After this, the Romans struggled to keep their empire together. By 407 it seems likely that most Roman troops had been withdrawn to help protect Rome itself from attack. In 410 the British asked Rome for military help but were told that they could not expect any. There was now little to stop the Saxons invading.

Over to you

- Copy the map into your folder and mark the routes of the different invader groups.
- Imagine you are one of the invading Saxons. Write a diary of your journey and what happens when you first arrive in Britain.

Everyday life in Saxon Britain

The Romans left behind well-built towns with houses made from stone and brick. The newly arrived Saxons ignored these completely and built their own small villages close to the land they began to farm.

The homes they built were made from local materials. A wooden frame was erected and then the walls filled in with either more wood or wattle and daub, a woven arrangement of sticks covered with mud and straw. The roof was then covered with either straw or reeds. The village often had a large hall in the centre where everyone could meet. This was where the chief of the village would live.

Strip farming

Farming land was shared out so that everyone had some good land as well as poorer land. Each family was allocated strips of land within each field. The Saxons used a rotation system. This meant that a different crop was grown in each field each year so that the land stayed fertile. One year they might grow barley and the next year wheat. The third year it would lie fallow – nothing was planted and animals were allowed to graze. In this way everyone was able to grow enough food for their families.

This is what a Saxon village would have looked like.

Work around the year

In spring the fields were ploughed and seed planted. Ploughs were heavy and needed at least four oxen to pull them. The oxen were probably shared by the villagers.

At the end of summer the harvest was brought in and stored for the winter. This was back-breaking work which involved everyone. A poor harvest meant that the villagers might starve during the winter.

In autumn the animals who could not be fed during the winter would be killed to provide meat for the months ahead. The meat was put into barrels and covered with salt to stop it going completely rotten.

Inside a Saxon home

Unlike the clean and airy houses of the Romans, the Saxon hut was dark and smoky. A fire burnt permanently in the centre of the one-room building, but there were no windows or chimneys to let the smoke out – it just seeped out through the thatched roof. In some houses animals shared the space with the family – just a simple partition separated them.

On the floor was either beaten earth or wooden boards. In some homes the floor was dug out and wooden planks placed over it. These absorbed any rising dampness from the ground. There was little furniture inside Saxon homes, perhaps just a few stools and a table.

Over to you

- Find some pictures of different Saxon homes. Do they all look the same? Draw some for your project folder.
- Design a Saxon house for a king: no expense spared, but no brick or stone to be used!

Family life

Life for Saxon families was difficult and full of dangers, but, with a little luck and much hard work, everyone would survive to see another summer. Although men and women did different work, everyone would join in at times of need. When the men were away fighting or trading, for example, the women and children would have had to manage all the farmwork. One difficulty we have in trying to establish the roles within the family was that all the writers of the time were male monks, who wrote very little about normal family life.

Men were under a bond of allegiance to their local chief. In return for the protection a strong chief could offer, each man was obliged to work and, if necessary, fight for him. This bond lasted for life.

Work for most men began as soon as the sun rose. There were animals to take care of and farm work to do. Getting fields ready for planting, weeding the growing crops and harvesting took most of the year. In addition there were building repairs to do and wood to cut for the fire. Finally the village fence had to be kept in good order.

Women worked just as hard. Besides looking after the children, they did most of the work inside the home. They kept the fire alive and cooked meals in a large pot hanging over the fire. They made the family's clothes. Wool was spun to make cloth, and plant dyes used to colour it. Women also made most of the butter, cheese and ale which the family needed. It is likely that elderly women were seen as the real head of their families, the figure of authority.

There were no schools for children to go to, but they had little time to play. Small children helped with jobs around the home. Older girls learnt to make butter and cheese, and how to sew and weave, and would also look after the younger children. As soon as boys were strong enough to be of use outside they helped look after the animals and worked in the fields, perhaps scaring birds away and looking out for wolves.

Did you know?

- An ordinary Saxon home measured about 19 metres by 7 metres and would have needed about 18 large oak trees for its construction.
- The only buildings the Saxons made from stone were their churches.
- Most villages were surrounded by a high fence to keep out wild animals and thieves.
- There were no rabbits in Saxon England! Can you find out why?

This illustration from a decorated manuscript shows a Saxon woman milking a cow.

The coming of Christianity

The Saxons who settled in England brought with them their own gods. These gods needed sacrifices and it is possible that this sometimes involved taking human lives. The Romans had been mainly Christian when they left, and it was not long before some decided to return to convert the people of England back to the faith.

In 596 Pope Gregory instructed his friend Augustine to lead a small group of about 20 monks on the long, dangerous journey to Britain. They arrived in Kent early in 597 and were taken to the king, Aethelbert. Fortunately for Augustine, Aethelbert had recently married Bertha, a French princess who was already a Christian. He agreed to listen to Augustine, and within a short time he was baptised. Many of Aethelbert's court also became Christians.

This is how Aethelbert replied to Augustine's first sermon, according to Bede, an eighth-century monk and writer.

'Your words and promises are fair indeed. But they are new and strange to us and I cannot accept them and throw away the age-old beliefs of the whole English nation. But since you have travelled so far … we will not harm you. We will receive you with friendship … and we will not stop you preaching and converting people to your faith.'

Within a hundred years all the Saxon kingdoms had accepted the Christian faith. But there were serious differences between the Celtic Christians and the followers of the Church in Rome. In 663 leaders of both sides met at Whitby to resolve these differences. The result was an agreement to obey the Church in Rome. This decision increased the links between England and mainland Europe, but it caused problems hundreds of years later.

The early Christians made beautiful jewellery to celebrate their faith.

Did you know?

- All the books produced during this period were written and illustrated by hand.
- It was only in the monasteries that children could learn to read and write.
- The church of St Martin in Canterbury, used by Augustine, had been built by Roman Christians more than 200 years earlier. Parts of the Roman church still remain.

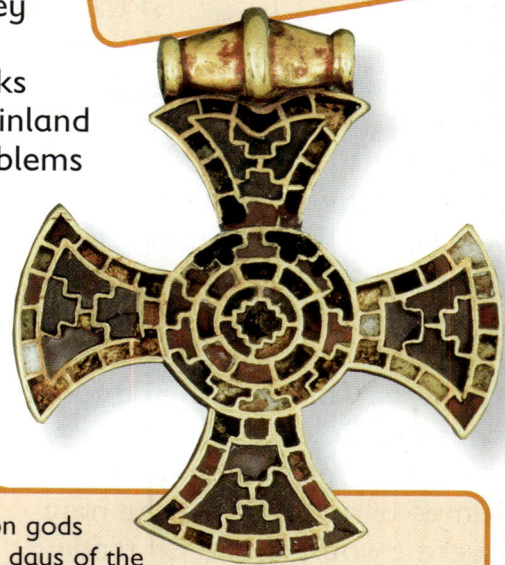

Over to you

The names of some of the Saxon gods still live on in our words for the days of the week. Draw pictures to show what you think these gods might have looked like, then try to find some pictures to see if you were right.

- Tiwesdaeg (Tiw's day) — the Saxon god of war, justice and peace treaties.
- Wodnesdaeg (Woden's day) — the chief god of the Saxons.
- Thursdaeg (Thor's day) -- the thunder god, and son of Woden.
- Frigedaeg (Frigga's day) — the wife of Woden, goddess of fertility.

Can you find out who the other days are named after? What about the months of the year?

The Sutton Hoo ship burial

In 1939 archaeologists working at Sutton Hoo, in Suffolk, opened a burial mound and discovered the remains of a complete ship burial. The boat had rotted away but its shape was still quite clear. Within the ship was treasure fit for a king. After all the excavations were finished a great mystery remained: whose burial was it? No traces of a body have ever been found, but coins within the site suggested that it might be Raedwald, a king of the East Anglians. There is no certainty, however, that this was his memorial.

Raedwald was one of the most powerful kings of his time. Bede tells us that he killed King Aethelbert of Kent and became chief of the English kings. He died in about 624. It is possible that the burial mound at Sutton Hoo is his, although the coins found there were made so close in time to his death that it may be that the burial belongs to a later king. Raedwald was converted to Christianity, but then went back to the old Saxon gods. Objects connected with both religions were found at Sutton Hoo.

Make a museum display

In the middle pages you will find pictures of some of the many artefacts that were found in the ship. Carefully cut out the pictures and mount them on card. Put a piece of Blu-Tack at the bottom of each artefact so that it can stand up.

For each artefact make a small card which gives the name and a brief explanation of what it is. Information about each one is given on page 10. You could even make a display case to keep all the exhibits in. If you do this, decorate the case so that it looks attractive. Finally, write an introductory paragraph for your display, explaining the significance of the Sutton Hoo ship. You could stand this card beside the display case. (Some ideas on how to make a display case are given on page 10.)

Note: remember to photocopy this page and page 10 before you cut out the shapes on pages 8 and 9.

Shield decoration

Purse lid

Shoulder clasp

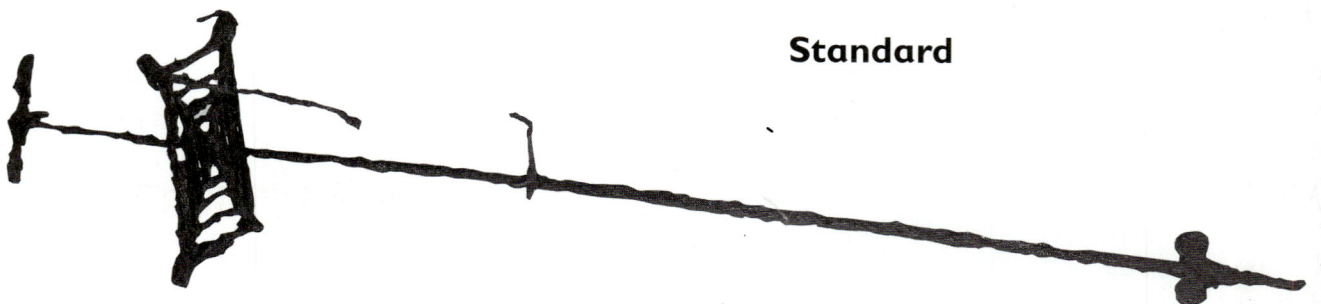

Helmet

Standard

Gold buckle

Sceptre

Silver spoons and bowls

Sword

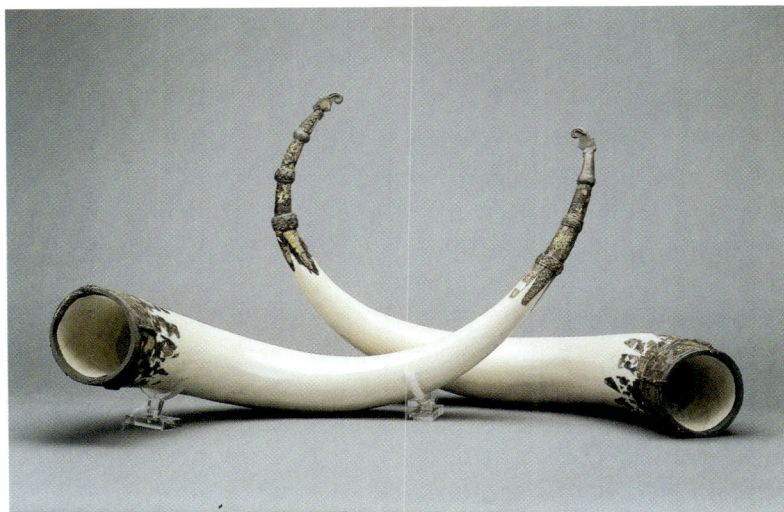

Drinking horns

How to make the display case

You will need a small, shallow box. (The sort used for apples would be suitable – try your local supermarket.) Cover the inside and the outside of the box with plain paper. You could decorate the paper with pictures of Saxon scenes, or a Saxon-style pattern.

Stick the pictures of the artefacts and their labels to the bottom of the inside of the box, so that when the box is standing upright they will be facing the viewer. When you have done this, cover the open side of the box with cling-film and stand it up with one of the long sides at the bottom.

Helmet

The helmet is one of the great finds of Sutton Hoo. It was decorated with iron and bronze and clearly belonged to an important king. There are various battle scenes shown on the panels. The amount of decoration suggests that the helmet was for ceremonial purposes only.

Shield

The limewood shield had rotted away, but what remained were the magnificent fittings with which the shield had been decorated. Although it was chiefly of practical use, the shield might also have had a ceremonial function.

Standard

This mysterious object has been interpreted as a kind of 'standard', a symbol of the king which might be carried into battle. Nothing like this has been found anywhere else.

Sceptre

The sceptre is a clear symbol of kingly authority. The Celtic heads carved at the top and bottom may have had magical properties.

Sword

The pattern-welded sword was one of the finest that Saxon craftsmen could create. It was made by twisting thin rods of iron together and then adding a cutting edge of high-carbon steel. The gold and jewelled decorations indicate that this belonged to a powerful king.

Drinking horns

Although almost all the ivory had disappeared, the silver decorations remain to suggest two magnificent drinking horns. They clearly belonged to someone of great wealth and importance: the craftsmanship of the silver work is amongst the finest ever found.

Purse lid

In amongst gold coins which it must have contained, was a richly decorated purse cover. Inlaid with semi-precious stones, it is an object of great beauty.

Gold buckle

Clothes were left in a neatly folded pile. Although the cloth has mostly disappeared, the decorated gold buckle is one of the most beautiful objects to survive from Saxon times.

Silver spoons and bowls

Although small, these are of great significance. The spoons have Christian inscriptions, which suggests that they belonged to a king who had been converted to the new faith.

Shoulder clasp

This beautiful object would have held the king's cloak on his shoulder. It is an exceptional example of Saxon craftsmanship.

The Anglo-Saxon Chronicle

The Anglo-Saxon Chronicle is a collection of writings begun during the reign of King Alfred. They record the history of Britain from the time of Christ, although these early writings are not reliable. Later events, recorded in the Chronicle soon after they happened, are more accurate.

The Chronicle was written by monks, so much of what it records is to do with the Church. But it gives us a fascinating insight into the minds of the people of this period. Here are a few extracts:

678 – There appeared the star called a comet, in August, and it shone for three months each morning like a beam of the sun.

685 – King Ecgferth was killed by the north sea, and a great host with him, on May 20th; he had been king for fifteen years. There was in Britain a bloody rain, and milk and butter turned to blood.

793 – In this year fierce, foreboding omens came over the land of Northumbria, and wretchedly terrified the people. There were excessive whirlwinds, lightning storms and fiery dragons were seen flying in the sky. These signs were followed by great famine, and shortly after in the same year, on January 8th, the ravaging of heathen men destroyed God's church at Lindisfarne through brutal robbery and slaughter.

865 – The heathen force stayed in Thanet, and accepted peace from the Kentish; the Kentish promised them money for the truce. Beside the promise of money, the army stole up by night and ravaged all of eastern Kent.

875 – That summer, king Alfred went out on the sea with a ship-force and fought with the companies of seven ships; they seized one and put the others to flight.

This page from an Anglo-Saxon gospel shows the beautiful and intricate work of the hand-written texts of this time.

Over to you

- Copy some of the extracts into your book and illustrate them in the style of the Saxon writers. Imagine what other events might have happened at this time and make up a few entries of your own, using the same style of writing.
- Try to read some more of the Chronicle (see the website box below). Do you think it is an accurate record of the period? What problems might historians have with this document?
- Make some decorated letter patterns using your own initials.

Other sources

www.sunsite.berkeley.edu/Anglo/part1.htm
This website contains the whole text of the Chronicle. Click on SunSite Digital Collections and go down to The Online Medieval and Classical Library and choose the Anglo-Saxon Chronicle.

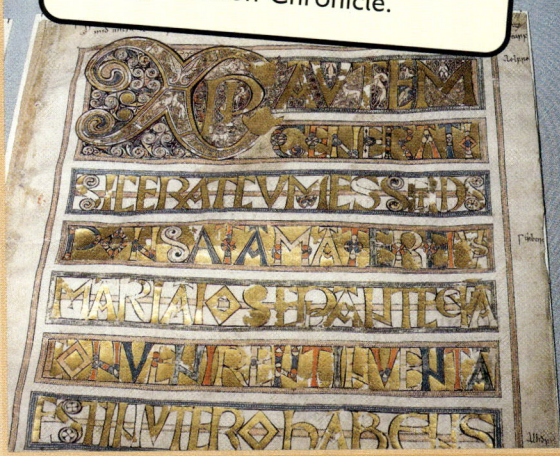

Of kings and kingdoms

There were seven kingdoms in Saxon England. They were often at war with one another and the borders constantly changed, depending on which kingdom was the most powerful. In the sixth century Kent was the strongest, but then Northumbria held power. Later Mercia emerged as the most powerful. By the time of the attacks by the Danes in the ninth century Wessex, under Alfred, had become the most important kingdom.

Ecgfrith

Ecgfrith was the last Northumbrian king to be the most powerful of all England. He became king in 670. He gave land and money to the new monasteries, including the one at Jarrow where the monk and writer Bede was to spend much of his life. Bede wrote about Ecgfrith, but not very favourably.

Ecgfrith was a warrior king who spent much of his life either planning invasions or trying to stop them. In 685 he led his army north to the land of the Picts. At Dunnichen Moss, in Forfar, the enemy pretended to run away and led Ecgfrith and his army into a narrow pass between the mountains. There they butchered the king and most of his army. The Northumbrians never attempted to expand their empire again.

Offa

One of the most powerful of the Saxon kings was Offa, king of Mercia from 757 to 796. He reigned over Northumbria, Wessex and Kent, and called himself Rex Anglorum – King of the English. One of his great achievements was the introduction of coins which everyone could rely on for weight and value.

His other lasting memorial is Offa's Dyke, a 120-mile-long embankment and ditch stretching between the rivers Severn and Dee. The dyke was built to mark the western edge of the Mercian border and to prevent Welsh raiders from attacking. It was built during the later part of Offa's reign, when his power was at its height. The fact that Offa could set his men to work on such a major building task indicates that it was a period of relative peace.

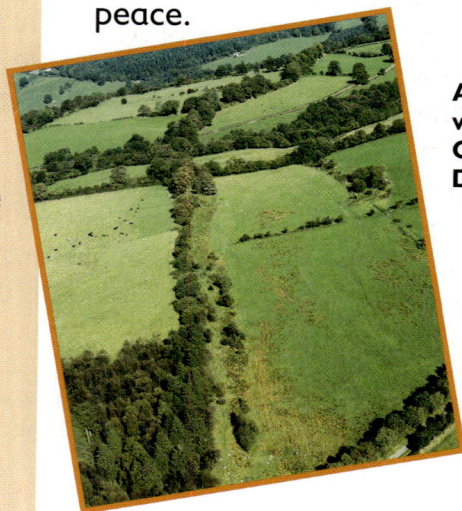

An aerial view of Offa's Dyke.

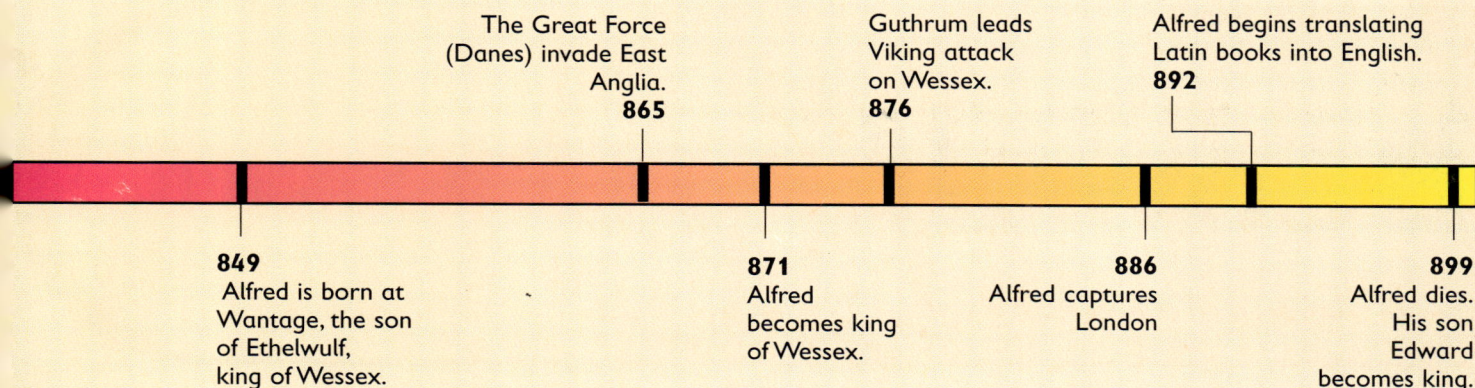

The Great Force
(Danes) invade East
Anglia.
865

Guthrum leads
Viking attack
on Wessex.
876

Alfred begins translating
Latin books into English.
892

849
Alfred is born at
Wantage, the son
of Ethelwulf,
king of Wessex.

871
Alfred
becomes king
of Wessex.

886
Alfred captures
London

899
Alfred dies.
His son
Edward
becomes king.

Alfred

The Saxon king Alfred is the only English monarch to have been given the title 'the Great'. By 878 the Danes, under their leader Guthrum, had been in England for ten years and were close to conquering the whole country. Only Alfred and the kingdom of Wessex stood against them. In January 878 they launched a surprise attack on Alfred's stronghold near Chippenham and the king was lucky to escape with his life. He hid, along with a few loyal followers, in the marshes around Athelney in Somerset, while the rest of Wessex submitted to Guthrum.

A few months later Alfred was ready to challenge the Danes. He gathered hundreds of men from the villages to join his army. At Edington, the two great armies met, but the battle was not decisive. Now Alfred showed what a wise leader he had become: he agreed a truce with Guthrum. In return for land in East Anglia and the north, Guthrum agreed not to attack Wessex and he was baptised a Christian. Alfred took hostages to make sure that Guthrum kept his word.

The two men agreed to meet again, at Wedmore in Somerset. Here Guthrum was baptised and Alfred became his godfather, which meant that the Dane now owed Alfred the allegiance due from an adopted son. By 880 the Danes had left Wessex and settled in the lands given to them. The part of England ruled by the Danes became known as the Danelaw.

The Danelaw

The army of Viking invaders who arrived in 865 were known as 'The Great Force'. Unlike previous raiders, they decided to stay in England over the winter and then spend the summer months attacking and stealing from Saxon settlements. Their leader was Guthrum. They nearly succeeded in conquering the whole country: only Wessex and part of Northumbria held out against the Great Force. Eventually Guthrum was forced to sign the Treaty of Wedmore which brought some peace to the war-torn country.

The Danelaw is the name given to that part of England which was under Danish control after 878. The area came under Danish law and the language spoken was Danish. Although there was an official peace, the Danes kept armed forces at several settlements such as Stamford, Derby and Lincoln. Many of the place names in these areas have Danish origins.

Over to you

- Imagine you can interview Alfred. Think of ten questions you could ask him. How might he have answered them?
- There is a famous object called 'The Alfred Jewel' in the Ashmolean Museum, Oxford. Find a picture of it, copy it into your book and write a few sentences about it. Design a jewel for Guthrum, the Danish leader.
- Alfred wrote many books himself. Try to find out more about them.

13

Beowulf

The Saxons were great storytellers. The few surviving stories and poems from this period are full of great adventures and heroic deeds. 'Beowulf' is the title of one of the best-known poems from this time. Here are a few short extracts.

The poem was probably written between 680 and 800 in the kingdom of Mercia. The story tells of a great hero, Beowulf, who battles against evil and who eventually loses his life. Beowulf fights Grendel, a monster who enjoys eating people. This is part of the description of Grendel taking away people to eat later!

At once that hellish monster,
grim and greedy, brutally cruel
started forward and seized thirty thanes
even as they slept; and then, gloating
over his plunder, he hurried from the hall,
made for his lair with all those slain warriors.

Here is part of Beowulf's fight with the monster. Grendel arrives in the great hall, after a feast, to find everyone asleep.

The monster was not disposed to delay;
but, for a start, he hungrily seized
a sleeping warrior, greedily wrenched him,
bit into his body, drank the blood
from his veins, devoured huge pieces;
until in no time, he had swallowed the whole man,
even his feet and hands.

New words
The word 'thane' means 'a companion of the king'. Use a dictionary to find out the meaning of any other words you don't know. Make a glossary of all these new words. (A glossary is a list of words with their meanings.)

Riddle
The Saxons loved to make up short riddles in the form of poems. Here is one for you to try. The answer is on page 15.

I'm by nature solitary, scarred by spear
and wounded by sword, weary of battle.
I frequently see the face of war, and fight
hateful enemies: yet I hold no hope
of help being brought to me in battle,
before I'm eventually done to death.
Who am I?

Beowulf wakes and grabs Grendel's arm as he reaches to take another sleeping warrior. A fight begins. Grendel realises that Beowulf is no ordinary man and tries to break free. But Beowulf does not know that no ordinary sword can hurt Grendel. Here is how the fight ends.

Beowulf held him fast,
he who was the strongest of all men
ever to have seen the light of life on earth.

The horrible monster
suffered grievous pain; a gaping wound
opened on his shoulder; the sinews sprang apart,
the muscles were bursting …
fatally wounded,
Grendel was obliged to make for the marshes,
head for his joyless lair.

What next?

Finishing your project

It is nearly time to finish this topic. You could go back now and look at the questions you asked at the start. Can you answer all of them? One way of finishing off the topic would be to have a final page in your folder headed 'What I have learnt about the Saxons?' On the page you could write and draw some of the many things you have learnt. You should also make a contents page at the beginning so that someone looking through your work will know exactly what to expect.

Websites

There are many websites where you will find information. Check these out:
www.bbc.co.uk/history/ancient/anglo saxons
www.thelighthouseforeducation.co.uk
www.romanremains.freeserve.co.uk/s.htm
The Education Zone at www.whsmith.co.uk

Did you know?

A Saxon no one knows much about!

Kenneth MacAlpin ruled the kingdom of Del Riata, on the west coast of Scotland. He was an ambitious man and by 843 had united all of what we now call Scotland. He made six attempts to extend his kingdom further south, into the land of the Angles, but never succeeded. When he died in 858, he had ruled a united Scotland for 16 years, during which time he had held the kingdom together despite regular Viking attacks. This was the first time that Scotland had been united as one country.

Places to visit

Many museums have something from this period, so check your local museum. There are lots of good places to go to see Saxon remains. Listed below are just a few of them. Don't leave it until the end of your project to make your visit. Try to go early on so that you can use the information you find out. Write up your visit and illustrate it with drawings and postcards. Don't forget to include your own thoughts about what you have learnt – this is often the most interesting part for someone else to read.

- South Cadbury, Somerset – possible site of Arthur's castle

- Durham Cathedral Museum – good material on the early English Church

- Jarrow – St Paul's Church, the ruin of Bede's monastery

- Lindisfarne Island – site of early monastery; one of the first to be attacked by Vikings

- The British Museum, London – a treasure store of Saxon and Viking artefacts, including the Sutton Hoo and Mildenhall artefacts

- Offa's Dyke – Saxon earthwork built between England and Wales

- Ashmolean Museum, Oxford – the Alfred Jewel plus many other interesting objects

- Wareham, Dorset – one of Alfred's burghs, which still has the original street plan and some defences visible

- West Stow, Suffolk – reconstructed Saxon village

- Winchester City Museum – good range of Saxon finds

- The Jorvik Centre, York – reconstruction of Viking York.

Over to you

Find out what you can about some of these other well-known people of Saxon times:
- Bede
- Aethelbert
- Edward the Confessor
- Augustine
- St Columba
- St Patrick
- Alcuin
- Charlemagne
- Aidan
- Cnut
- Earl Godwine

Answer to riddle on page 14
A shield

First published 2002 exclusively for WHSmith by

Hodder & Stoughton Educational
338 Euston Road
LONDON NW1 3BH

Text and illustrations © Hodder & Stoughton Educational 2002

All rights reserved.

A CIP record of this book is available from the British Library.

Text: Paul Flux
Illustrations: Neil Rogers
Developed by Topics, The Creative Partnership Ltd, Exeter.

ISBN 0 340 84730 1

10 9 8 7 6 5 4 3 2 1

Printed in Spain for Hodder & Stoughton Educational by Graphycems.

Acknowledgements
Photographs are reproduced by permission of:
Ancient Art & Architecture Collection: p.11;
Bridgeman Art Library: p.6, p.9 (sceptre), p.12 (coin); British Library: p.5; British Museum: p.7, p.8 (standard), p.9 (sword, drinking horns, silver spoons and bowls); Robert Harding Picture Library: p.2; Michael Holford: p.8 (helmet, shield, purse lid, shoulder clasp), p.9 (gold buckle); Skyscan Photolibrary: p.12 (Offa's Dyke).

WH S

AGE 7-11

project helpers

Saxons

WHSmith *Project Helpers*

Everything you need to create brilliant projects and spice up your homework!

Each helper contains:

- *How to do a project*
  Tips on planning your project and finding useful information

- *Fascinating facts, great ideas and fun activities*
  Bring your project to life!

- *Colour illustrations*
  Photographs and drawings that illuminate the text

At school, for homework or just for fun, use **WHSmith Project Helpers** for success every time.

Other titles in the **WHSmith Project Helpers** Series

ISBN 0-340-84730-1

£1.99

9 780340 847305